I do not claim
to be a great poet,
but a great observer of her.

To the readers

I do not know how the idea of putting short little
sentiments written for custom made hallmark cards,
became a best-selling book that blesses many
women living on this earth.
I am just glad that it did.

From the bottom of my heart,
thank you for loving & supporting **HER.**

Her.

Pierre Alex Jeanty

Jeanius
PUBLISHING

Cover Design: Omar Rodriguez
Editor: Carla DuPont Huger
Illustration: TreManda Pewett

ISBN-13: 978-1-949191-05-9

Jeanius Publishing LLC
430 Lee Blvd
Lehigh Acres, FL 33936

For more information, please visit:
Jeaniuspublishing.com
Pierrealexjeanty.com

Schools & Businesses

Jeanius Publishing books are available at quantity discounts
with bulk purchases.
For more information please email contact@jeaniuspublishing.com

She's a poetry book.
You must read every letter
and digest every word.
Every facet of her paints
a part of the bigger picture.
You can't love her
if you do not intend on
reading every page,
and learning how to
comprehend every piece of her.

You're love blooming;
an exceptional woman growing roots
in a field of women who aspire to be
bad girls and heartless savages.

There's nothing wrong with that.
There's no beauty in living life numbly
and holding hands with misery.

Therefore, continue being both the sun
and the moon.

Dear,

Your smile will be like
the sun cracking through the clouds
to the man of your dreams.

There is nothing
wrong with being
an old soul
waiting on
new love.

Women like her

are both salt and sugar;

how her love tastes

truthfully depends on

what you bring to the table,

and how you serve it.

You are more
than worthy of love.
However,
you will never be
worthy enough
to someone
who isn't worthy
of your love.

She is everything

a *man* will

desire and need,

as well as everything

a *boy* will not understand,

not value, and will

take for granted.

Do not expect her
to just get up and forgive.

Have you known anyone
who has been shot in the heart
and didn't bleed or
suffer from the pain it brings?

To demand that she acts like
it didn't hurt
and put it easily in the past,
is to ask her to be a robot,
rather than a human who feels.

Leave her to heal.

What good are flowers without water?
What good are promises without actions?

She wasn't created
for everybody,
and her heart wasn't
made for everyone.

Her love won't
be enough for
just any man.

You're priceless, not a dime.
Never exchange yourself for dollars.

You are far more than a diva.
Therefore, do not wrestle with the idea
of being a good woman in this life,
and then settle for being the "bad chick".

Perfect people
are just good pretenders
and exceptional liars.
To ask her to be perfect
is to ask her to be those things.

She is looking for a man
who will devote
less time questioning
why there are walls
around her heart,
and more time
jumping,
climbing,
breaking,
and doing whatever is necessary
to get past those walls.

Once upon a time,
persuasive words
would give her goosebumps,
and sweet nothings would satisfy her
cravings.
The keys to her heart belonged to thieves.

But now,
she has grown to listen with her eyes,
to only trust actions,
and to study behaviors.
She has allowed time to be the inspector,
to see what it will reveal.

She wants
to be loved with an
honest tongue,
devoted heart,
and exclusive eyes.

Women like her

are only hard to love

by men who believe

love is just a word.

Only people with big hearts
like yours find love.
Those with small hearts
cannot endure or persevere.

Small hearts do not leave room for love
once they've faced enough trial.
They become storage for bitterness and
resentment, without leaving space for
anything else.

It's not her shape,
her face, or her hair
that makes her beautiful.
It is neither the smoothness of her skin,
the boldness when she stands,
or the perseverance in her heart.
It is the condition of her heart,
the gratitude she lives by,
and her love for God
that expresses true beauty.

She can be difficult.
There are times her words
will be heavy with stubbornness,
her tongue will be sharper than a new
sword, and her attitude like that of a two-
year-old.

Aren't we all difficult at times?
Isn't she human like everyone else?

Love her

the way you crave

to be loved.

Maybe you should not have
given them so much of you.

Maybe you would have
never known what
love can taste like if you didn't.

Maybe, you would have never learned
that you could be enough for someone,
yet too much for them.

You may not be their cup of tea,
but to someone else,
you will be an entire ocean of everything
that quenches their thirst
and awakens their soul.

She isn't meant
to be handled
with caution,
but to be loved hard.

She is to be
passionate about,
caressed deep down
to her soul,
and understood
in her silence.

Love is not for those who like to pick
things up, and put them down when they
get bored.
Love is for the hoarders, who like to keep
even the smallest bit of meaning on their
"forever" shelves.
Love is for those who know how to hang
on and fight, until their arms can't lift
themselves anymore.

Hearts
aren't made
to be broken,
they are meant
to be fed love.

All she wants is for you
to love her during the days
she needs love the most.

Who isn't loveable when their world is
nothing but sunshine and rainbows?

Your love will never be too much
for anyone searching for something real.
Authentic love is only good bait for those
fishing for more than just a good catch.

You deserve

to be with someone

who searches

for the beautiful

things in you.

Her broken heart is searching
for a new reason to love again,
more than it is trying to find
a hand that will help it
get pieced back together.

It knows eventually
it'll become whole again, but it must
have the hope that once lived at the center
of it before it is restored.

She is far much more
than a good woman.

She is
a beautiful soul
who carries
light in her smile,
love in her bones,
and power within her skull.

How can you not be enough
when the oceans swear that
you are treasure to their eyes?

The sunset cannot compare, dear.
Must I remind you that the human eye
can only see so far and so much?

She has had
plenty of men
willing to give her
the world,
but none were willing
to make her their world.
So she waits...

If you thirst
for a love that
will drown all of the doubts
growing in your soul,
and the fear vacationing in your mind,

you must never settle
for someone who lacks passion
in their eyes when they stare at you.

Desiring a man
whose efforts speak
in a higher tone
than his promises,
isn't too much to ask for.

You will never amount to much
by forcing your image to become
identical to their reflection.
You are not them,
and they do not want to be you.
You must stay on your own path,
to keep yourself out of their lane.

She is
the same as wine;
without patience,
you will never
see how much better
she gets with time.

The pain will come.
Let it visit,
cry it out,
vent it out,
bleed it out.
And then ask it to leave.

Do not allow it to build a home
and call it broken.

We aren't meant to be broken forever.
That is punishment to our hearts and
minds.

Their loss of interest in you

doesn't make you

any less interesting.

Only a joker
can misdeal
a beautiful
heart, and
a queen
like you.

She's everything but crazy.
They've mistaken her passion
for aggressiveness,
her needs for silly demands,
and her standards for stubbornness.

Her flaws were too much for them to
endure. Her willingness to love without
condition and her demand for the same,
drove them away.

If you aren't willing
to love her,
do not put dents
in her heart
that will influence
her to believe that
she is hard to love.
That is cruel.

Pieces of you will still ask for her.
You will not be able to silence them by
introducing them to someone else's voice.

People like her are harder to forget
than they are to love.

She is far more than
what meets the eyes.
You will not recognize
how beautiful she is,
until you start looking
at the things the eyes can't see.

Do not judge
her by her past.

She is still having
dialogues with that
version of herself,
trying to figure out
what the heck
was wrong with her then.

Do not condemn her,
she already struggles to forgive herself.

Her type of woman is the type
for which your love will never run dry,
nor will your fear of love drive her away.

You'll never want to stop
making memories with her.

If their love becomes poison to you,
you've grabbed the wrong bottle.

She did not choose
to be alone,
she simply chose
to love herself more.
It required her
to be the love of her own life,
until someone
comes to fulfill that position.

The sun and the moon
take turns admiring her.
The sun watches her rise,
as it finds its way to
the other side of the world
to cover its next shift.
The moon tags in
to watch her sleep.

If you
cannot
swallow your pride,
you do not
have enough hunger
for a woman
like her;
you are not thirsty
enough for her love.

She is the most perfect illustration
of the word sexy.
Fascinating described her,
and gorgeous was her first name.

Whoever's last name she carries,
they should know that they've
been struck by luck.

If she cannot dance without care,
laugh and tell you about the most
embarrassing moments in her life,
she is not yet free in your presence.
Her heart is only yours when she is able to
undress her soul in your midst.

Dear Black Girl,

Your skin is a beautiful place to live in,
your hair is grass from the heavens, and
your shape is a beautiful sculpture.
You are not magic;
magic is only an illusion.
You are more than a miracle,
you are an unexpected blessing.

You owe no one an explanation
for being yourself,
Yes, be unapologetically you,
but you owe *yourself* an apology
if a better version of you
does not come alive in long periods of time.
You are meant to grow and evolve.

You're too powerful to be
a slave of acceptance.
Their compliments should not define you,
nor should their criticism break you.

As they say,
"Validation is only for parking."

She's been in many rings,
fighting for love alone and losing.

Yet, she waits for the one
who will see the champion in her,
the one who will give her a ring and
forever.

Love is meant to
blossom in the good,
and endure through the bad.

If it cannot persevere through the bad,
don't call it love.

The day you hold her,
you will feel as if you are carrying
the world and all the beauty in it.

That day, you will learn that
she is tender and innocent,
yet tough and full of fire.

She's far from the devil
they've claimed that she is.
They acted as Lucifer, while
demanding that
she give them heaven.
Heaven was made for angels,
it's not a good home
for those who resemble fallen ones.

Your love can only
be priceless to someone
who recognizes your worth.

If you do not
recognize this,
you too have not
recognized your worth.

The failed attempts were
only losing small battles.
You will win the war
when love becomes yours.

Do not let the small losses
keep you from the win that matters.

She hesitates
when it comes to opening up,
because she has fallen in love
too quickly before, and none of those
she fell for opened their arms to catch her.

Can you blame her for making sure that
your hands are big enough
to hold her heart,
your intentions are true enough
for your arms to open,
and you're strong enough to catch her?

Do not allow your heart to
be stolen by a man who doesn't
put up a good fight against oxygen for you;
one who won't stop taking
your breath away every occasion
that he gets.

The love you deserve

is meant to know forever.

Until you truly realize
that you are a queen,
jokers will invite themselves
into your heart,
masking themselves as kings.

She is meant to be loved
with every breath.
She has to be worth dying for,
for you to understand that.

If you ever find yourself
lost without them,
find your way home.

And if their heart is no longer home,
find who you were before them.

Don't dare her to be different,

she already is.

Dare her to be herself.

Your love is like liquor,
strong enough
to cause any man willing
to drink all of you
to become drunk in love.

If loving them means
not loving you,
it is not love,
but lust playing
its trick on you.

When you look at her,
if you do not feel
blessed to have her,
she is not yours to keep.
She is another man's blessing.

If they have yet
to fall in love
with your naked soul,
your naked body
should not be available
for them to make love to.

To her past,

I see you replaying the worst scenes
of her life over and over,
trying to convince her
that she is less than good.

Listen to me,
I will love her until you
become a memory faded,
until your words are without sound
and empty to her ears.

I will love her until
you no longer get the best of her,
until you are nothing to her.

She shouldn't have to
change to be a recipient
of your love.

Only ask her to be yours, and
be by her side as she changes.

That's the way to love
and grow with her.

Maybe it wasn't love,

maybe it was

what you wanted it to be.

She desired consistency,
and substance that would
quench her thirst
for something true;
someone loyal,
with a passion
that would end
her hunger for love.

Her worth is priceless,
and she is fully aware of it .
It's the reason why she doesn't attract
many,
and only those with quality taste
and genuine hearts
can afford a woman like her.

She is used to good dogs
and bad boys.
There is nothing different
about the two.
Good dogs are usually bad boys,
and bad boys behave like good dogs.
She longs for the day when
she can find a good one in both.

Love doesn't knock,
it comes like a tornado,
looking to blow away the walls
around your heart
and leave you open and vulnerable.

She can sometimes
be the thunder
while life rains on you.
Don't expect her to
always be the calm.

If you need to be certain about anything,
it is that she will always be
the rainbow and the sunshine after.

God took his time on you.

You're proof that His most

beautiful design is a woman.

She is strong,
but when you hold her,
know that she is fragile.
Be gentle,
speak soft words to her,
and slowly run your fingers through her
hair.
Hold her as if she is a newborn,
and it's the first time
that you've laid eyes on her.

Darling,

You must put how he treats you before
how much he pleases you.
You can't make love to someone who only
has only fed you versions of hate.

She's a tree,
and her fruits of love
will never come into fruition
if you do not water her.
Pour affection, attention,
communication, and motivation
on her roots.

You both were
once strangers
looking for love,
and now
you are both strangers
afraid of love.

She chases after her dreams
as if she is running for her life.
Don't get in the way
if you won't help her reach them.

How many women like her
do you know, live as if life is nothing
if they don't become something?

Her ear craves,
"I love you,"
from a voice that makes her
feel secure and valued.

She needs to be loved deeply
and her inner beauty
ought to be treasured,
but never forget to remind her that
she is beautiful on the surface.

There's no stronger poison
to a woman's heart,
than a man with sweet words
and bitter actions.
It keeps many women
bittersweet about love.

The sun rises behind her smile
and the sunset is in her eyes.

Broken hearts
can still love
and broken people
are still loveable.

If you do not love yourself,
others will use that to
justify their inability to love you.

To describe her
is to write
sweet poetry
about the
beauty of life
and survival.

You shouldn't
lose sleep
over someone
who was only
a nightmare to you.

There will be nothing
beautiful about waking up
next to someone like that.

Her beauty can only be
compared to the heavens.

There will be times you will have
to be your own friend and lover,
your own shoulder to cry on,
and use your own hands to wipe your
tears.
Those times will feel lonely,

but they will teach you how to stand on
your own when no one has your back.

People have a strange way
of telling you that they are guilty;
they will start by acting as if they are not.

If we do not drop
the weight
of our past,
misery will await us
at every stop on our journey.

It'll be heavy,
it'll smell,
and it'll be loud.

Haven't you seen miserable people?
They aren't that hard to recognize.

You can't
keep trying to
suck the love
out of someone
who sucks at love,
especially if they
do not intend on
changing that.

She has a lot to bring to the table.
She is her own provider,
and has accomplished many things
on her own strength.

When you come into her life,
offer your help and provide it
whether she freely accepts it or not.

She is independent,
but that doesn't mean she doesn't
like having someone
she can depend on.

You are perfect
the way you are,
without a perfect body,
perfect hair,
or perfect skin.
Your imperfections
are what make
you perfect to love.

There are very few things

as adventurous

as exploring her mind.

Her heart is covered
by layers of pain.
It is love that will
peel the layers off,
and trust that will bring
the walls down.

Trust her and love her,
and do not forget it won't be possible
without patience.

Perhaps breakups
are such tragedies
because we give so much
to people who weren't meant
to be candidates for our love,
yet we chose them anyway.

She is a mermaid,
going against the flow.
The wave society expects
her to follow
tries to drown her true identity .
Enslaved she no longer wants to be, but
free to be who she needs to be.

We want to be understood,
our hearts to be treasured,
and to be loved
for who we truly are.

They say love is blind,
but she isn't invisible.

Maybe they're blind,
and this love is too much
for their eyes to capture.

Love is a marathon,
but she kept running into sprinters;
those who wanted her prize,
but weren't willing to go the distance.

Maybe they were fools,
or maybe their endurance wasn't built to
pursue a woman like her.

If a man gives her room to,
her love will pierce his ego
and destroy the false ideologies
of manhood in his life.

She is art
in a beautiful museum
we recognize to be this world.
Although she was beautiful,
sophisticated, and captivating,
not every one cared to appreciate that.

And that's okay.

The moment she didn't
want to be fooled anymore,
was when he chose not to
be a fool anymore.
The beauty of bad timing.

Love is a miracle
that happens
to those who believe.

Don't stop believing.

Her defensive ways
are safety checks
for those trying to
enter her heart.

She was a brave soul,
a rebel at heart,
unwilling to be a "love-hater"
despite the failures
and the circumstances
she had met on her love journey.

Somehow, she remained a believer
and lover despite the trail of blood that
followed her from the leaking of unhealed
wounds, stabbed back, and cut heart.

She loves him
more than he'll ever know,
and he loves her
more than he'll ever show.

What a tragedy.

Her skin is made
out of the finest silk,
with the smell of Eden
and the taste of honey.

She wants a love
that will not cage
her independence
and hold hostage
her dreams,
but contribute to her freedom.

To her Ex,

I will never thank you
for continually stabbing her heart,
beating it as if it were a drum, rather than
protecting it as if it were fragile.
However, I will acknowledge you
for making her strong.
Because you let her down so often, she
had to learn how to stand up for herself.
Because of you, I have me a strong woman.

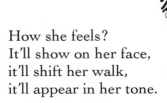

How she feels?
It'll show on her face,
it'll shift her walk,
it'll appear in her tone.

You will learn that
her body language doesn't lie,
and her lips will say things that
 aren't truly how she feels.

It'll help you know what she isn't saying,
when she is saying something.

Your love
is the ocean,
and the man for you
will dive as deep
as it takes
to reach the
undiscovered
parts of you.

I cannot tell you how to love

a woman like her,

but I can tell you half-hearted love

won't do it.

Fight for her
by fighting with her,
when she is in the ring
fighting for
the relationship.

You don't let a
fighter like her go.

You are your own kind of beautiful.
Be that kind of beautiful.
Be both kind and beautiful.

The man for you
will understand that
you are both a survivor and a warrior,
full of scars, yet fearless.

She refused to become a slave to the false
opinions they uttered about her,
and trained her ears to be deaf to the false
assumptions and accusations they spread.

That's what made her powerful;
nothing irrelevant could keep her attention.

Do not kiss her with lying lips,
nor french kiss her with a sharp
tongue and a deceitful heart.

That is a crime.

Love
should
not
cost
you
your
sanity.

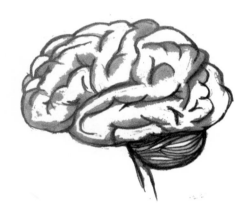

If you cannot serve her your heart,
do not set a table of hope for her.
Do not serve her lies and
feed her false promises.

She's a lioness,
with a wild heart
and a strong mind.
Fire burns in her bones,
while love flows
through her veins.

Convince her with effort,
and love her with your heart.
Words and promises do not hold enough
weight to convince her anymore.

Pierre Alex Jeanty

Another word for beautiful is,
"be yourself."
Be yourself my dear,
it's a beautiful thing.

You can learn so much about
her by exploring her scars, and asking
about her fears.

She is still guarded
because many thieves came in before,
broke her trust,
and held her mind hostage.
She is still trying to break free.

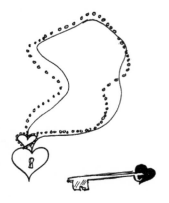

Isn't it ironic that the perfect moment for them to admit that they need you in their life, is when you finally realize that you're well off without them?

In other words,
the devil knows when you are getting close to heaven.

If only you picked your man
in the same manner
you choose which selfie to post,
which outfit to wear,
or which restaurant to eat at.

Being picky can help secure
the right pick at times.

Beware, there are some who will come to
play the role of being a good partner.
They don't want your heart,
they are merely auditioning for other parts
of you.

She doesn't believe
in settling anymore.
In her eyes, it is signing
a contract with disappointment
and begging to be taken for granted.
The girl who once settled,
no longer lives in the same flesh as her.

She is more than a perfect dimension.
She stays in shape because she is in love
with being a well-rounded person.
If you see her perfect shape before you
look at her perfectly shaped heart,
you will miss so much.

If love lives on your tongue
and shows itself in your speech,
yet doesn't own your heart,
it is dead. It is nothing but ashes
pretending to be fire.

She's more than medicine
to a man's hormones,
more than something to satisfy
his natural needs.

Her body is more than an object,
it is a beautiful temple
where God's princess calls home.
It is the bed of a leader,
and the pillow of an angelic being.

People are just people,
some are poison,
some are sweet.
We aren't all the same.
We aren't all good or bad.

To let a woman
like her go freely,
is to prove that you are a fool
who doesn't know the true
treasures of this life.

You have to love the parts of her
that aren't easy to love,
and the parts of her that others
and even herself have struggled to love,
to see how beautiful loving her will be.

Perhaps if you wait
for a husband
and stop treating
boyfriends as princes.
you will no longer kiss the wrong frogs.

Pierre Alex Jeanty

Please understand that closure will
not come when you walk away.
You will only find it
when you find a reason to stay away.

Guard your heart,
but do not make it a
forbidden place to everyone.
There will be people who are
worthy of entry.

She didn't need a hero,
she didn't need to be rescued,
she needed something different
from the bad she had known.
She wanted a man whose mouth
wasn't full of half-truths,
and whose heart wasn't crippled by the
fear of commitment.

In a generation of people who want to be
heartless, savages, and empty of feelings,
it'll be hard to find someone
who is what you need.
But do not become like the world.

Be loyal, be truthful, be emotional, and be
full of feelings. Be hungry for love, be
thirsty for affection, and anything else
human beings ought to desire.

Let them be foolish and cold.
Don't dim your light
to become as dark as they are.

147

You shouldn't feel ugly
because the ones who had you
couldn't appreciate
the beautiful things about you.

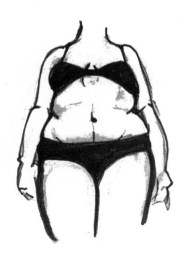

There is no greater
revenge against
someone who shattered
your heart into pieces,
than letting go
and opening the door
for something good
to walk into your life
when the time is right.

If he only knew
how sexy consistency
was to her,
and how beautiful vulnerability
was in her eyes,
he would not get too comfortable.

You were rare

before they knew what diamonds were,

way before they knew that beautiful is a

person rather than a word.

Thank You

About the Author

Pierre Alex Jeanty, Founder of Gentlemenhood™ and CEO of Jeanius Publishing, is a Haitian-American author, poet, and influencer, who is devoted to making an impact through his writing. He primarily focuses on poetically sharing his journey, lessons, and mistakes along the paths of manhood and love. Pierre vows to share his wisdom with all, in hopes of inspiring men to become better, and to be a voice of hope to women who have lost faith in good men. This is the vision of his brand, and the agenda he follows as a writer.

Pierre currently resides in southwest Florida with his family and travels as a speaker as he continues to write.

You can contact him through pierrealexjeanty.com
And find him on
Instagram: PierreJeanty
Facebook: Pierre Alex Jeanty
Twitter: PierreAJeanty
and other social networks by searching his name.